Morals of the Catholic Church

Morals of the Catholic Church

St. Augustine

Morals of the Catholic Church
© Lighthouse Publishing 2017

Written by: St. Augustine (Nov.13 354 – Aug.28 430)

Translated by: Rev. Richard Stothert, M.A.

Updated into Modern U.S English by A.M. Overett (b. 1960)

All rights reserved. Without limiting the rights under copyright reserved above, no part of this publication may be reproduced, stored in a retrieval system, or transmitted, in any form or by any means (electronic, mechanical, photocopying, recording or otherwise), without the prior written permission of the copyright owner of this book.

Published by
Lighthouse Christian Publishing
SAN 257-4330
5531 Dufferin Drive
Savage, Minnesota, 55378
United States of America

www.lighthousechristianpublishing.com

Introductory Notice.

It is laid down at the outset that the customs of the holy life of the Church should be referred to the chief good of man, that is, God. We must seek after God with supreme affection; and this doctrine is supported in the Catholic Church by the authority of both Testaments. The four virtues get their names from different forms of this love. Then follow the duties of love to our neighbor. In the Catholic Church we find examples of continence and of true Christian conduct.

Chapter 1.—How the Pretensions of the Manichæans are to Be Refuted. Two Manichæan Falsehoods.

1. Enough, probably, has been done in our other books in the way of answering the ignorant and profane attacks which the Manichæans make on the law, which is called the Old Testament, in a spirit of vainglorious boasting, and with the approval of the uninstructed. Here, too, I may shortly touch upon the subject. For everyone with average intelligence can easily see that the explanation of the Scriptures should be sought for from those who are the professed teachers of the Scriptures; and that it may happen, and indeed always happens, that many things seem absurd to the ignorant, which, when they are explained by the learned, appear all the more excellent, and are received in the explanation with the greater pleasure because the obstructions which made it difficult to reach the meaning. This commonly happens as regards the holy books of the Old Testament, if only the man who meets with difficulties applies to a pious teacher, and not to a profane critic, and if he begins his inquiries from a desire to find truth, and not in rash opposition. And should the inquirer meet with some, whether bishops or presbyters, or any officials or ministers of the Catholic Church, who either avoid in all cases opening up mysteries, or, content with simple faith, have no desire for more recondite knowledge, he must not despair of finding the knowledge of the truth in a case where neither are all able to teach to whom the inquiry is addressed, nor are all inquirers worthy of learning the truth. Diligence and piety are both necessary: on the one

hand, we must have knowledge to find truth, and, on the other hand, we must deserve to get the knowledge.

2. But as the Manichæans have two tricks for catching the unwary, so as to make them take them as teachers,—one, that of finding fault with the Scriptures, which they either misunderstand or wish to be misunderstood, the other, that of making a show of chastity and of notable abstinence,—this book shall contain our doctrine of life and morals according to Catholic teaching, and will perhaps make it appear how easy it is to pretend to virtue, and how difficult to possess virtue. I will refrain, if I can, from attacking their weak points, which I know well, with the violence with which they attack what they know nothing of; for I wish them, if possible, to be cured rather than conquered. And I will quote such testimonies from the Scriptures as they are bound to believe, for they shall be from the New Testament; and even from this I will take none of the passages which the Manichæans when hard pressed are accustomed to call spurious, but passages which they are obliged to acknowledge and approve. And for every testimony from apostolic teaching I will bring a similar statement from the Old Testament, that if they ever become willing to wake up from their persistent dreams, and to rise towards the light of Christian faith, they may discover both how far from being Christian is the life which they profess, and how truly Christian is the Scripture which they cavil at.

Chapter 2.—He Begins with Arguments, in Compliance with the Mistaken Method of the Manichæans.

3. Where, then, shall I begin? With authority, or with reasoning? In the order of nature, when we learn anything, authority precedes reasoning. For a reason may seem weak, when, after it is given, it requires authority to confirm it. But because the minds of men are obscured by familiarity with darkness, which covers them in the night of sins and evil habits, and cannot perceive in a way suitable to the clearness and purity of reason, there is most wholesome provision for bringing the dazzled eye into the light of truth under the congenial shade of authority. But since we have to do with people who are perverse in all their thoughts and words and actions, and who insist on nothing more than on beginning with argument, I will, as a concession to them, take what I think a wrong method in discussion. For I like to imitate, as far as I can, the gentleness of my Lord Jesus Christ, who took on Himself the evil of death itself, wishing to free us from it.

Chapter 3.—Happiness is in the Enjoyment of Man's Chief Good. Two Conditions of the Chief Good: 1st, Nothing is Better Than It; 2d, It Cannot Be Lost Against the Will.

4. How then, according to reason, ought man to live? We all certainly desire to live happily; and there is no human being but assents to this statement almost before it is made. But the title happy cannot, in my opinion, belong either to him who has not what he loves,

whatever it may be, or to him who has what he loves if it is hurtful or to him who does not love what he has, although it is good in perfection. For one who seeks what he cannot obtain suffers torture, and one who has got what is not desirable is cheated, and one who does not seek for what is worth seeking for is diseased. Now in all these cases the mind cannot but be unhappy, and happiness and unhappiness cannot reside at the same time in one man; so in none of these cases can the man be happy. I find, then, a fourth case, where the happy life exists,—when that which is man's chief good is both loved and possessed. For what do we call enjoyment but having at hand the objects of love? And no one can be happy who does not enjoy what is man's chief good, nor is there anyone who enjoys this who is not happy. We must then have at hand our chief good, if we think of living happily.

5. We must now inquire what is man's chief good, which of course cannot be anything inferior to man himself. For whoever follows after what is inferior to himself, becomes himself inferior. But every man is bound to follow what is best. Wherefore man's chief good is not inferior to man. Is it then something similar to man himself? It must be so, if there is nothing above man which he can enjoy. But if we find something which is both superior to man, and can be possessed by the man who loves it, who can doubt that in seeking for happiness man should endeavor to reach that which is more excellent than the being who makes the endeavor. For if happiness consists in the enjoyment of a good than which there is nothing better, which we call the chief good, how can a man be properly called happy who has not yet attained to his chief good? or how can that be the chief

good beyond which something better remains for us to arrive at? Such, then, being the chief good, it must be something which cannot be lost against the will. For no one can feel confident regarding a good which he knows can be taken from him, although he wishes to keep and cherish it. But if a man feels no confidence regarding the good which he enjoys, how can he be happy while in such fear of losing it?

Chapter 4.—Man—What?

6. Let us then see what is better than man. This must necessarily be hard to find, unless we first ask and examine what man is. I am not now called upon to give a definition of man. The question here seems to me to be,—since almost all agree, or at least, which is enough, those I have now to do with are of the same opinion with me, that we are made up of soul and body,—What is man? Is he both of these? or is he the body only, or the soul only? For although the things are two, soul and body, and although neither without the other could be called man (for the body would not be man without the soul, nor again would the soul be man if there were not a body animated by it), still it is possible that one of these may be held to be man, and may be called so. What then do we call man? Is he soul and body, as in a double harness, or like a centaur? Or do we mean the body only, as being in the service of the soul which rules it, as the word lamp denotes not the light and the case together, but only the case, yet it is on account of the light that it is so called? Or do we mean only the mind, and that on account of the body which it rules, as horseman means not the man and the horse, but the man only, and that as

employed in ruling the horse? This dispute is not easy to settle; or, if the proof is plain, the statement requires time. This is an expenditure of time and strength which we need not incur. For whether the name man belongs to both, or only to the soul, the chief good of man is not the chief good of the body; but what is the chief good either of both soul and body, or of the soul only, that is man's chief good.

Chapter 5.—Man's Chief Good is Not the Chief Good of the Body Only, But the Chief Good of the Soul.

7. Now if we ask what is the chief good of the body, reason obliges us to admit that it is that by means of which the body comes to be in its best state. But of all the things which invigorate the body, there is nothing better or greater than the soul. The chief good of the body, then, is not bodily pleasure, not absence of pain, not strength, not beauty, not swiftness, or whatever else is usually reckoned among the goods of the body, but simply the soul. For all the things mentioned the soul supplies to the body by its presence, and, what is above them all, life. Hence, I conclude that the soul is not the chief good of man, whether we give the name of man to soul and body together, or to the soul alone. For as according to reason, the chief good of the body is that which is better than the body, and from which the body receives vigor and life, so whether the soul itself is man, or soul and body both, we must discover whether there is anything which goes before the soul itself, in following which the soul comes to the perfection of good of which it is capable in its own kind. If such a thing can be found, all uncertainty must be at an end, and we must pronounce this to be really and

truly the chief good of man.

8. If, again, the body is man, it must be admitted that the soul is the chief good of man. But clearly, when we treat of morals,—when we inquire what manner of life must be held in order to obtain happiness,—it is not the body to which the precepts are addressed, it is not bodily discipline which we discuss. In short, the observance of good customs belongs to that part of us which inquires and learns, which are the prerogatives of the soul; so, when we speak of attaining to virtue, the question does not regard the body. But if it follows, as it does, that the body which is ruled over by a soul possessed of virtue is ruled both better and more honorably, and is in its greatest perfection in consequence of the perfection of the soul which rightfully governs it, that which gives perfection to the soul will be man's chief good, though we call the body man. For if my coachman, in obedience to me, feeds and drives the horses he has charge of in the most satisfactory manner, himself enjoying the more of my bounty in proportion to his good conduct, can anyone deny that the good condition of the horses, as well as that of the coachman, is due to me? So the question seems to me to be not, whether soul and body is man, or the soul only, or the body only, but what gives perfection to the soul; for when this is obtained, a man cannot but be either perfect, or at least much better than in the absence of this one thing.

Chapter 6.—Virtue Gives Perfection to the Soul; The Soul Obtains Virtue by Following God; Following God is the Happy Life.

9. No one will question that virtue gives perfection to the soul. But it is a very proper subject of inquiry whether this virtue can exist by itself or only in the soul. Here again arises a profound discussion, needing lengthy treatment; but perhaps my summary will serve the purpose. God will, I trust, assist me, so that, notwithstanding our feebleness, we may give instruction on these great matters briefly as well as intelligibly. In either case, whether virtue can exist by itself without the soul, or can exist only in the soul, undoubtedly in the pursuit of virtue the soul follows after something, and this must be either the soul itself, or virtue, or something else. But if the soul follows after itself in the pursuit of virtue, it follows after a foolish thing; for before obtaining virtue it is foolish. Now the height of a follower's desire is to reach that which he follows after. So the soul must either not wish to reach what it follows after, which is utterly absurd and unreasonable, or, in following after itself while foolish, it reaches the folly which it flees from. But if it follows after virtue in the desire to reach it, how can it follow what does not exist? or how can it desire to reach what it already possesses? Either, therefore, virtue exists beyond the soul, or if we are not allowed to give the name of virtue except to the habit and disposition of the wise soul, which can exist only in the soul, we must allow that the soul follows after something else in order that virtue may be produced in itself; for neither by following after nothing, nor by following after folly, can the soul, according to my reasoning, attain to wisdom.

10. This something else then, by following after which the soul becomes possessed of virtue and wisdom, is either a wise man or God. But we have said already that it must be something that we cannot lose against our will. No one can think it necessary to ask whether a wise man, supposing we are content to follow after him, can be taken from us despite our unwillingness or our persistence. God then remains, in following after whom we live well, and in reaching whom we live both well and happily. If any deny God's existence, why should I consider the method of dealing with them, when it is doubtful whether they ought to be dealt with at all? At any rate, it would require a different starting-point, a different plan, a different investigation from what we are now engaged in. I am now addressing those who do not deny the existence of God, and who, moreover, allow that human affairs are not disregarded by Him. For there is no one, I suppose, who makes any profession of religion but will hold that divine Providence cares at least for our souls.

Chapter 7.—The Knowledge of God to Be Obtained from the Scripture. The Plan and Principal Mysteries of the Divine Scheme of Redemption.

11. But how can we follow after Him whom we do not see? or how can we see Him, we who are not only men, but also men of weak understanding? For though God is seen not with the eyes but with the mind, where can such a mind be found as shall, while obscured by foolishness, succeed or even attempt to drink in that light? We must therefore have recourse to the instructions of those whom we have reason to think wise.

Thus far argument brings us. For in human things reasoning is employed, not as of greater certainty, but as easier from use. But when we come to divine things, this faculty turns away; it cannot behold; it pants, and gasps, and burns with desire; it falls back from the light of truth, and turns again to its wonted obscurity, not from choice, but from exhaustion. What a dreadful catastrophe is this, that the soul should be reduced to greater helplessness when it is seeking rest from its toil! So, when we are hasting to retire into darkness, it will be well that by the appointment of adorable Wisdom we should be met by the friendly shade of authority, and should be attracted by the wonderful character of its contents, and by the utterances of its pages, which, like shadows, typify and attemper the truth.

12. What more could have been done for our salvation? What can be more gracious and bountiful than divine providence, which, when man had fallen from its laws, and, in just retribution for his coveting mortal things, had brought forth a mortal offspring, still did not wholly abandon him? For in this most righteous government, whose ways are strange and inscrutable, there is, by means of unknown connections established in the creatures subject to it, both a severity of punishment and a mercifulness of salvation. How beautiful this is, how great, how worthy of God, in fine, how true, which is all we are seeking for, we shall never be able to perceive, unless, beginning with things human and at hand, and holding by the faith and the precepts of true religion, we continue without turning from it in the way which God has secured for us by the separation of the patriarchs, by the bond of the law, by the foresight of the prophets, by the witness of the apostles, by the blood of the martyrs,

and by the subjugation of the Gentiles. From this point, then, let no one ask me for my opinion, but let us rather hear the oracles, and submit our weak inferences to the announcements of Heaven.

Chapter 8.—God is the Chief Good, Whom We are to Seek After with Supreme Affection.

13. Let us see how the Lord Himself in the gospel has taught us to live; how, too, Paul the apostle,—for the Manichæans dare not reject these Scriptures. Let us hear, O Christ, what chief end Thou dost prescribe to us; and that is evidently the chief end after which we are told to strive with supreme affection. "Thou shalt love," He says, "the Lord thy God." Tell me also, I pray Thee, what must be the measure of love; for I fear lest the desire enkindled in my heart should either exceed or come short in fervor. "With all thy heart," He says. Nor is that enough. "With all thy soul." Nor is it enough yet. "With all thy mind." What do you wish more? I might, perhaps, wish more if I could see the possibility of more. What does Paul say on this? "We know," he says, "that all things issue in good to them that love God." Let him, too, say what is the measure of love. "Who then," he says, "shall separate us from the love of Christ? shall tribulation, or distress, or persecution, or famine, or nakedness, or peril, or the sword?" We have heard, then, what and how much we must love; this we must strive after, and to this we must refer all our plans. The perfection of all our good things and our perfect good is God. We must neither come short of this nor go beyond it: the one is dangerous, the other impossible.

Chapter 9.—Harmony of the Old and New Testament on the Precepts of Charity.

14. Come now, let us examine, or rather let us take notice,—for it is obvious and can be seen, at once,—whether the authority of the Old Testament too agrees with those statements taken from the gospel and the apostle. What need to speak of the first statement, when it is clear to all that it is a quotation from the law given by Moses? For it is there written, "Thou shalt love the Lord thy God with all thy heart, and with all thy soul, and with all thy mind." And not to go farther for a passage of the Old Testament to compare with that of the apostle, he has himself added one. For after saying that no tribulation, no distress, no persecution, no pressure of bodily want, no peril, no sword, separates us from the love of Christ, he immediately adds, "As it is written, For Thy sake we are in suffering all the day long; we are accounted as sheep for the slaughter." The Manichæans are in the habit of saying that this is an interpolation,—so unable are they to reply, that they are forced in their extremity to say this. But everyone can see that this is all that is left for men to say when it is proved that they are wrong.

15. And yet I ask them if they deny that this is said in the Old Testament, or if they hold that the passage in the Old Testament does not agree with that of the apostle. For the first, the books will prove it; and as for the second, those prevaricators who fly off at a tangent will be brought to agree with me, if they will only reflect a little and consider what is said, or else I will press upon them the opinion of those who judge impartially. For what could agree more harmoniously than these passages? For tribulation, distress, persecution, famine,

nakedness, peril, cause great suffering to man while in this life. So all these words are implied in the single quotation from the law, where it is said, "For Thy sake we are in suffering." The only other thing is the sword, which does not inflict a painful life, but removes whatever life it meets with. Answering to this are the words, "We are accounted as sheep for the slaughter." And love could not have been more plainly expressed than by the words, "For Thy sake." Suppose, then, that this testimony is not found in the Apostle Paul, but is quoted by me, must you not prove, you heretic, either that this is not written in the old law, or that it does not harmonize with the apostle? And if you dare not say either of these things (for you are shut up by the reading of the manuscript, which will show that it is written, and by common sense, which sees that nothing could agree better with what is said by the apostle), why do you imagine that there is any force in accusing the Scriptures of being corrupted? And once more, what will you reply to a man who says to you, This is what I understand, this is my view, this is my belief, and I read these books only because I see that everything in them agrees with the Christian faith? Or tell me at once if you will venture deliberately to tell me to the face that we are not to believe that the apostles and martyrs are spoken of as having endured great sufferings for Christ's sake, and as having been accounted by their persecutors as sheep for the slaughter? If you cannot say this, why should you bring a charge against the book in which I find what you acknowledge I ought to believe?

Chapter 10.—What the Church Teaches About God. The Two Gods of the Manichæans.

16. Will you say that you grant that we are bound to love God, but not the God worshipped by those who acknowledge the authority of the Old Testament? In that case you refuse to worship the God who made heaven and earth, for this is the God set forth all through these books. And you admit that the whole of the world, which is called heaven and earth, had God and a good God for its author and maker. For in speaking to you about God we must make a distinction. For you hold that there are two gods, one good and the other bad. But if you say that you worship and approve of worshipping the God who made heaven and earth, but not the God supported by the authority of the Old Testament, you act impertinently in trying, though vainly, to attribute to us views and opinions altogether unlike the wholesome and profitable doctrine we really hold. Nor can your silly and profane discourses be at all compared with the expositions in which learned and pious men of the Catholic Church open up those Scriptures to the willing and worthy. Our understanding of the law and the prophets is quite different from what you suppose. Mistake us no longer. We do not worship a God who repents, or is envious, or needy, or cruel, or who takes pleasure in the blood of men or beasts, or is pleased with guilt and crime, or whose possession of the earth is limited to a little corner of it. These and such like are the silly notions you are in the habit of denouncing at great length. Your denunciation does not touch us. The fancies of old women or of children you attack with a vehemence that is only ridiculous. Anyone whom you persuade in this way to

join you shows no fault in the teaching of the Church, but only proves his own ignorance of it.

17. If, then, you have any human feeling,—if you have any regard for your own welfare,—you should rather examine with diligence and piety the meaning of these passages of Scripture. You should examine, unhappy beings that you are; for we condemn with no less severity and copiousness any faith which attributes to God what is unbecoming Him, and in those by whom these passages are literally understood we correct the mistake of ignorance, and look upon persistence in it as absurd. And in many other things which you cannot understand there is in the Catholic teaching a check on the belief of those who have got beyond mental childishness, not in years, but in knowledge and understanding—old in the progress towards wisdom. For we learn the folly of believing that God is bounded by any amount of space, even though infinite; and it is held unlawful to think of God, or any part of Him, as moving from one place to another. And should anyone suppose that anything in God's substance or nature can suffer change or conversion, he will be held guilty of wild profanity. There are thus among us children who think of God as having a human form, which they suppose He really has, which is a most degrading idea; and there are many of full age to whose mind the majesty of God appears in its inviolableness and unchangeableness as not only above the human body, but above their own mind itself. These ages, as we said, are distinguished not by time, but by virtue and discretion. Among you, again, there is no one who will picture God in a human form; but neither is there one who sets God apart from the contamination of human error. About those who are fed like crying babies at the breast of the

Catholic Church, if they are not carried off by heretics, they are nourished according to the vigor and capacity of each, and arrive at last, one in one way and another in another, first to a perfect man, and then to the maturity and hoary hairs of wisdom, when they may get life as they desire, and life in perfect happiness.

Chapter 11.—God is the One Object of Love; Therefore He is Man's Chief Good. Nothing is Better Than God. God Cannot Be Lost Against Our Will.

18. Following after God is the desire of happiness; to reach God is happiness itself. We follow after God by loving Him; we reach Him, not by becoming entirely what He is, but in nearness to Him, and in wonderful and immaterial contact with Him, and in being inwardly illuminated and occupied by His truth and holiness. He is light itself; we get enlightenment from Him. The greatest commandment, therefore, which leads to happy life, and the first, is this: "Thou shalt love the Lord thy God with all thy heart, and soul, and mind." For to those who love the Lord all things issue in good. Hence Paul adds shortly after, "I am persuaded that neither death, nor life, nor angels, nor virtue, nor things present, nor things future, nor height, nor depth, nor any other creature, shall be able to separate us from the love of God, which is in Christ Jesus our Lord." If, then, to those who love God all things issue in good, and if, as no one doubts, the chief or perfect good is not only to be loved, but to be loved so that nothing shall be loved better, as is expressed in the words, "With all thy soul, with all thy heart, and with all thy mind," who, I ask, will not at once conclude, when these things are all settled and

most surely believed, that our chief good which we must hasten to arrive at in preference to all other things is nothing else than God? And then, if nothing can separate us from His love, must not this be surer as well as better than any other good?

19. But let us consider the points separately. No one separates us from this by threatening death. For that with which we love God cannot die, except in not loving God; for death is not to love God, and that is when we prefer anything to Him in affection and pursuit. No one separates us from this in promising life; for no one separates us from the fountain in promising water. Angels do not separate us; for the mind cleaving to God is not inferior in strength to an angel. Virtue does not separate us; for if what is here called virtue is that which has power in this world, the mind cleaving to God is far above the whole world. Or if this virtue is perfect rectitude of our mind itself, this in the case of another will favor our union with God, and in ourselves will itself unite us with God. Present troubles do not separate us; for we feel their burden less the closer we cling to Him from whom they try to separate us. The promise of future things does not separate us; for both future good of every kind is surest in the promise of God, and nothing is better than God Himself, who undoubtedly is already present to those who truly cleave to Him. Height and depth do not separate us; for if the height and depth of knowledge are what is meant, I will rather not be inquisitive than be separated from God; nor can any instruction by which error is removed separate me from Him, by separation from whom it is that anyone is in error. Or if what is meant are the higher and lower parts of this world, how can the promise of heaven separate me from Him who

made heaven? Or who from beneath can frighten me into forsaking God, when I should not have known of things beneath but by forsaking Him? In fine, what place can remove me from His love, when He could not be all in every place unless He were contained in none?

Chapter 12.—We are United to God by Love, in Subjection to Him.

20. "No other creature," he says, separates us. O man of profound mysteries! He thought it not enough to say, no creature: but he says no other creature; teaching that with which we love God and by which we cleave to God, our mind, namely, and understanding, is itself a creature. Thus the body is another creature; and if the mind is an object of intellectual perception, and is known only by this means, the other creature is all that is an object of sense, which as it were makes itself known through the eyes, or ears, or smell, or taste, or touch, and this must be inferior to what is perceived by the intellect alone. Now, as God also can be known by the worthy, only intellectually, exalted though He is above the intelligent mind as being its Creator and Author, there was danger lest the human mind, from being reckoned among invisible and immaterial things, should be thought to be of the same nature with Him who created it, and so should fall away by pride from Him to whom it should be united by love. For the mind becomes like God, to the extent vouchsafed by its subjection of itself to Him for information and enlightenment. And if it obtains the greatest nearness by that subjection which produces likeness, it must be far removed from Him by that presumption which would make the likeness greater. It is

this presumption which leads the mind to refuse obedience to the laws of God, in the desire to be sovereign, as God is.

21. The farther, then, the mind departs from God, not in space, but in affection and lust after things below Him, the more it is filled with folly and wretchedness. So by love it returns to God,—a love which places it not along with God, but under Him. And the more ardor and eagerness there is in this, the happier and more elevated will the mind be, and with God as sole governor it will be in perfect liberty. Hence it must know that it is a creature. It must believe what is the truth,—that its Creator remains ever possessed of the inviolable and immutable nature of truth and wisdom, and must confess, even in view of the errors from which it desires deliverance, that it is liable to folly and falsehood. But then again, it must take care that it be not separated by the love of the other creature, that is, of this visible world, from the love of God Himself, which sanctifies it in order to lasting happiness. No other creature, then,—for we are ourselves a creature,—separates us from the love of God which is in Christ Jesus our Lord.

Chapter 13.—We are Joined Inseparably to God by Christ and His Spirit.

22. Let this same Paul tell us who is this Christ Jesus our Lord. "To them that are called," he says, "we preach Christ the virtue of God, and the wisdom of God." And does not Christ Himself say, "I am the truth?" If, then, we ask what it is to live well,—that is, to strive after happiness by living well,—it must assuredly be to love virtue, to love wisdom, to love truth, and to love with all

the heart, with all the soul, and with all the mind; virtue which is inviolable and immutable, wisdom which never gives place to folly, truth which knows no change or variation from its uniform character. Through this the Father Himself is seen; for it is said, "No man cometh unto the Father but by me." To this we cleave by sanctification. For when sanctified we burn with full and perfect love, which is the only security for our not turning away from God, and for our being conformed to Him rather than to this world; for "He has predestinated us," says the same apostle, "that we should be conformed to the image of His Son."

23. It is through love, then, that we become conformed to God; and by this conformation, and configuration, and circumcision from this world we are not confounded with the things which are properly subject to us. And this is done by the Holy Spirit. "For hope," he says, "does not confound us; for the love of God is shed abroad in our hearts by the Holy Spirit, which is given unto us." But we could not possibly be restored to perfection by the Holy Spirit, unless He Himself continued always perfect and immutable. And this plainly could not be unless He were of the nature and of the very substance of God, who alone is always possessed of immutability and invariableness. "The creature," it is affirmed, not by me but by Paul, "has been made subject to vanity." And what is subject to vanity is unable to separate us from vanity, and to unite us to the truth. But the Holy Spirit does this for us. He is therefore no creature. For whatever is, must be either God or the creature.

Chapter 14.—We Cleave to the Trinity, Our Chief Good, by Love.

24. We ought then to love God, the Trinity in unity, Father, Son, and Holy Spirit; for this must be said to be God Himself, for it is said of God, truly and in the most exalted sense, "Of whom are all things, by whom are all things, in whom are all things." Those are Paul's words. And what does he add? "To Him be glory." All this is exactly true. He does not say, To them; for God is one. And what is meant by, To Him be glory, but to Him be chief and perfect and widespread praise? For as the praise improves and extends, so the love and affection increases in fervor. And when this is the case, mankind cannot but advance with sure and firm step to a life of perfection and bliss. This, I suppose, is all we wish to find when we speak of the chief good of man, to which all must be referred in life and conduct. For the good plainly exists; and we have shown by reasoning, as far as we were able, and by the divine authority which goes beyond our reasoning, that it is nothing else but God Himself. For how can anything be man's chief good but that in cleaving to which he is blessed? Now this is nothing but God, to whom we can cleave only by affection, desire, and love.

Chapter 15.—The Christian Definition of the Four Virtues.

25. As to virtue leading us to a happy life, I hold virtue to be nothing else than perfect love of God. For the fourfold division of virtue I regard as taken from four forms of love. For these four virtues (would that all felt

their influence in their minds as they have their names in their mouths!), I should have no hesitation in defining them: that temperance is love giving itself entirely to that which is loved; fortitude is love readily bearing all things for the sake of the loved object; justice is love serving only the loved object, and therefore ruling rightly; prudence is love distinguishing with sagacity between what hinders it and what helps it. The object of this love is not anything, but only God, the chief good, the highest wisdom, the perfect harmony. So we may express the definition thus: that temperance is love keeping itself entire and incorrupt for God; fortitude is love bearing everything readily for the sake of God; justice is love serving God only, and therefore ruling well all else, as subject to man; prudence is love making a right distinction between what helps it towards God and what might hinder it.

Chapter 16.—Harmony of the Old and New Testaments.

26. I will briefly set forth the manner of life according to these virtues, one by one, after I have brought forward, as I promised, passages from the Old Testament parallel to those I have been quoting from the New Testament. For is Paul alone in saying that we should be joined to God so that there should be nothing between to separate us? Does not the prophet say the same most aptly and concisely in the words, "It is good for me to cleave to God?" Does not this one word cleave express all that the apostle says at length about love? And do not the words, It is good, point to the apostle's statement, "All things issue in good to them that love

God?" Thus in one clause and in two words the prophet sets forth the power and the fruit of love.

27. And as the apostle says that the Son of God is the virtue of God and the wisdom of God,—virtue being understood to refer to action, and wisdom to teaching (as in the gospel these two things are expressed in the words, "All things were made by Him," which belongs to action and virtue; and then, referring to teaching and the knowledge of the truth, he says, "The life was the light of men"),—could anything agree better with these passages than what is said in the Old Testament of wisdom, "She reaches from end to end in strength, and orders all things sweetly?" For reaching in strength expresses virtue, while ordering sweetly expresses skill and method. But if this seems obscure, see what follows: "And of all," he says, "God loved her; for she teaches the knowledge of God, and chooses His works." Nothing more is found here about action; for choosing works is not the same as working, so this refers to teaching. There remains action to correspond with the virtue, to complete the truth we wish to prove. Read then what comes next: "But if," he says, "the possession which is desired in life is honorable, what is more honorable than wisdom, which works all things?" Could anything be brought forward more striking or more distinct than this, or even more fully expressed? Or, if you wish more, hear another passage of the same meaning. "Wisdom," he says, "teaches sobriety, and justice, and virtue." Sobriety refers, I think, to the knowledge of the truth, or to teaching; justice and virtue to work and action. And I know nothing comparable to these two things, that is, to efficiency in action and sobriety in contemplation, which the virtue of God and the wisdom of God, that is, the Son of God, gives to them

that love Him, when the same prophet goes on to show their value; for it is thus stated: "Wisdom teaches sobriety, and justice, and virtue, than which nothing is more useful in life to man."

28. Perhaps some may think that those passages do not refer to the Son of God. What, then, is taught in the following words: "She displays the nobility of her birth, having her dwelling with God?" To what does birth refer but to parentage? And does not dwelling with the Father claim and assert equality? Again, as Paul says that the Son of God is the wisdom of God, and as the Lord Himself says, "No man knows the Father save the only begotten Son," what could be more concordant than those words of the prophet: "With Thee is wisdom which knows Thy works, which was present at the time of Thy making the world, and knew what would be pleasing in Thine eyes?" And as Christ is called the truth, which is also taught by His being called the brightness of the Father (for there is nothing round about the sun but its brightness which is produced from it), what is there in the Old Testament more plainly and obviously in accordance with this than the words, "Thy truth is round about Thee?" Once more, Wisdom herself says in the gospel, "No man cometh unto the Father but by me;" and the prophet says, "Who knows Thy mind, unless Thou gives wisdom?" and a little after, "The things pleasing to Thee men have learned, and have been healed by wisdom."

29. Paul says, "The love of God is shed abroad in our hearts by the Holy Spirit which is given unto us;" and the prophet says, "The Holy Spirit of knowledge will shun guile." For where there is guile there is no love. Paul says that we are "conformed to the image of the Son of God;" and the prophet says, "The light of Thy countenance is

stamped upon us." Paul teaches that the Holy Spirit is God, and therefore is no creature; and the prophet says, "Thou sends Thy Spirit from the higher." For God alone is the highest, than whom nothing is higher. Paul shows that the Trinity is one God, when he says, "To Him be glory;" and in the Old Testament it is said, "Hear, O Israel, the Lord thy God is one God."

Chapter 17.—Appeal to the Manichæans, Calling on Them to Repent.

30. What more do you wish? Why do you resist ignorantly and obstinately? Why do you pervert untutored minds by your mischievous teaching? The God of both Testaments is one. For as there is an agreement in the passages quoted from both, so is there in all the rest, if you are willing to consider them carefully and impartially. But because many expressions are undignified, and so far adapted to minds creeping on the earth, that they may rise by human things to divine, while many are figurative, that the inquiring mind may have the more profit from the exertion of finding their meaning, and the more delight when it is found, you pervert this admirable arrangement of the Holy Spirit for the purpose of deceiving and ensnaring your followers. As to the reason why divine Providence permits you to do this, and as to the truth of the apostle's saying, "There must needs be many heresies, that they which are approved may be made manifest among you," it would take long to discuss these things, and you, with whom we have now to do, are not capable of understanding them. I know you well. To the consideration of divine things, which are far higher than you suppose, you bring minds quite gross and sickly,

from being fed with material images.

31. We must therefore in your case try not to make you understand divine things, which is impossible, but to make you desire to understand. This is the work of the pure and guileless love of God, which is seen chiefly in the conduct, and of which we have already said much. This love, inspired by the Holy Spirit, leads to the Son, that is, to the wisdom of God, by which the Father Himself is known. For if wisdom and truth are not sought for with the whole strength of the mind, it cannot possibly be found. But when it is sought as it deserves to be, it cannot withdraw or hide itself from its lovers. Hence its words, which you too are in the habit of repeating, "Ask, and ye shall receive; seek, and ye shall find; knock, and it shall be opened unto you:" "Nothing is hid which shall not be revealed." It is love that asks, love that seeks, love that knocks, love that reveals, love, too, that gives continuance in what is revealed. From this love of wisdom, and this studious inquiry, we are not debarred by the Old Testament, as you always say most falsely, but are exhorted to this with the greatest urgency.

32. Hear, then, at length, and consider, I pray you, what is said by the prophet: "Wisdom is glorious, and never faded away; yea, she is easily seen of them that love her, and found of such as seek her. She prevented them that desire her, in making herself first known unto them. Whoso seeks her early shall have no great travail; for he shall find her sitting at his doors. To think, therefore, upon her is perfection of wisdom; and whoso watches for her shall quickly be without care. For she goes about seeking such as are worthy of her, shows herself favorably unto them in the ways, and meets them in every thought. For the very true beginning of her is the desire

of discipline; and the care of discipline is love; and love is the keeping of her laws; and the giving heed unto her laws is the assurance of incorruption; and incorruption makes us near unto God. Therefore, the desire of wisdom brings to a kingdom." Will you still continue in dogged hostility to these things? Do not things thus stated, though not yet understood, make it evident to everyone that they contain something deep and unutterable? Would that you could understand the things here said! Forthwith you would abjure all your silly legends and your unmeaning material imaginations, and with great alacrity, sincere love, and full assurance of faith, would betake yourselves bodily to the shelter of the most holy bosom of the Catholic Church.

Chapter 18.—Only in the Catholic Church is Perfect Truth Established on the Harmony of Both Testaments.

33. I could, according to the little ability I have, take up the points separately, and could expound and prove the truths I have learned, which are generally more excellent and lofty than words can express; but this cannot be done while you bark at it. For not in vain is it said, "Give not that which is holy to dogs." Do not be angry. I too barked and was a dog; and then, as was right, instead of the food of teaching, I got the rod of correction. But were there in you that love of which we are speaking, or should it ever be in you as much as the greatness of the truth to be known requires, may God vouchsafe to show you that neither is there among the Manichæans the Christian faith which leads to the summit of wisdom and truth, the attainment of which is the true

happy life, nor is it anywhere but in the Catholic teaching. Is not this what the Apostle Paul appears to desire when he says, "For this cause I bow my knees to the Father of our Lord Jesus Christ, from whom the whole family in heaven and earth is named, that He would grant unto you, according to the riches of His glory, to be strengthened with might by His Spirit in the inner man: that Christ may dwell in your hearts by faith; that ye, being rooted and grounded in love, may be able to comprehend with all saints what is the height, and length, and breadth, and depth, and to know the love of Christ, which passes knowledge, that ye may be filled with all the fullness of God?" Could anything be more plainly expressed?

34. Wake up a little, I beseech you, and see the harmony of both Testaments, making it quite plain and certain what should be the manner of life in our conduct, and to what all things should be referred. To the love of God we are incited by the gospel, when it is said, "Ask, seek, knock;" by Paul, when he says, "That ye, being rooted and grounded in love, may be able to comprehend;" by the prophet also, when he says that wisdom can easily be known by those who love it, seek for it, desire it, watch for it, think about it, care for it. The salvation of the mind and the way of happiness is pointed out by the concord of both Scriptures; and yet you choose rather to bark at these things than to obey them. I will tell you in one word what I think. Do you listen to the learned men of the Catholic Church with as peaceable a disposition, and with the same zeal, that I had when for nine years I attended on you: there will be no need of so long a time as that during which you made a fool of me. In a much, a very much, shorter time you will see the

difference between truth and vanity.

Chapter 19.—Description of the Duties of Temperance, According to the Sacred Scriptures.

35. It is now time to return to the four virtues, and to draw out and prescribe a way of life in conformity with them, taking each separately. First, then, let us consider temperance, which promises us a kind of integrity and incorruption in the love by which we are united to God. The office of temperance is in restraining and quieting the passions which make us pant for those things which turn us away from the laws of God and from the enjoyment of His goodness, that is, in a word, from the happy life. For there is the abode of truth; and in enjoying its contemplation, and in cleaving closely to it, we are assuredly happy; but departing from this, men become entangled in great errors and sorrows. For, as the apostle says, "The root of all evils is covetousness; which some having followed, have made shipwreck of the faith, and have pierced themselves through with many sorrows." And this sin of the soul is quite plainly, to those rightly understanding, set forth in the Old Testament in the transgression of Adam in Paradise. Thus, as the apostle says, "In Adam we all die, and in Christ we shall all rise again." Oh, the depth of these mysteries! But I refrain; for I am now engaged not in teaching you the truth, but in making you unlearn your errors, if I can, that is, if God aid my purpose regarding you.

36. Paul then says that covetousness is the root of all evils; and by covetousness the old law also intimates that the first man fell. Paul tells us to put off the old man and put on the new. By the old man he means Adam who

sinned, and by the new man him whom the Son of God took to Himself in consecration for our redemption. For he says in another place, "The first man is of the earth, earthy; the second man is from heaven, heavenly. As is the earthy, such are they also that are earthy; and as is the heavenly, such are they also that are heavenly. And as we have borne the image of the earthy, let us also bear the image of the heavenly," —that is, put off the old man, and put on the new. The whole duty of temperance, then, is to put off the old man, and to be renewed in God,—that is, to scorn all bodily delights, and the popular applause, and to turn the whole love to things divine and unseen. Hence that following passage which is so admirable: "Though our outward man perish, our inward man is renewed day by day." Hear, too, the prophet singing, "Create in me a clean heart, O God, and renew a right spirit within me." What can be said against such harmony except by blind barkers?

Chapter 20.—We are Required to Despise All Sensible Things, and to Love God Alone.

37. Bodily delights have their source in all those things with which the bodily sense comes in contact, and which are by some called the objects of sense; and among these the noblest is light, in the common meaning of the word, because among our senses also, which the mind uses in acting through the body, there is nothing more valuable than the eyes, and so in the Holy Scriptures all the objects of sense are spoken of as visible things. Thus, in the New Testament we are warned against the love of these things in the following words: "While we look not at the things which are seen, but at the things which are

not seen; for the things which are seen are temporal, but the things which are not seen are eternal." This shows how far from being Christians those are who hold that the sun and moon are to be not only loved but worshipped. For what is seen if the sun and moon are not? But we are forbidden to regard things which are seen. The man, therefore, who wishes to offer that incorrupt love to God must not love these things too. This subject I will inquire into more particularly elsewhere. Here my plan is to write not of faith, but of the life by which we become worthy of knowing what we believe. God then alone is to be loved; and all this world, that is, all sensible things, are to be despised,—while, however, they are to be used as this life requires.

Chapter 21.—Popular Renown and Inquisitiveness are Condemned in the Sacred Scriptures.

38. Popular renown is thus slighted and scorned in the New Testament: "If I wished," says St. Paul, "to please men, I should not be the servant of Christ." Again, there is another production of the soul formed by imaginations derived from material things, and called the knowledge of things. About this we are fitly warned against inquisitiveness to correct which is the great function of temperance. Thus it is said, "Take heed lest anyone seduce you by philosophy." And because the word philosophy originally means the love and pursuit of wisdom, a thing of great value and to be sought with the whole mind, the apostle, with great prudence, that he might not be thought to deter from the love of wisdom, has added the words, "And the elements of this world." For some people, neglecting virtues, and ignorant of what

God is, and of the majesty of nature which remains always the same, think that they are engaged in an important business when searching with the greatest inquisitiveness and eagerness into this material mass which we call the world. This begets so much pride, that they look upon themselves as inhabitants of the heaven of which they often discourse. The soul, then, which purposes to keep itself chaste for God must refrain from the desire of vain knowledge like this. For this desire usually produces delusion, so that the soul thinks that nothing exists but what is material; or if, from regard to authority, it confesses that there is an immaterial existence, it can think of it only under material images, and has no belief regarding it but that imposed by the bodily sense. We may apply to this the precept about fleeing from idolatry.

39. To this New Testament authority, requiring us not to love anything in this world, especially in that passage where it is said, "Be not conformed to this world,"—for the point is to show that a man is conformed to whatever he loves,—to this authority, then, if I seek for a parallel passage in the Old Testament, I find several; but there is one book of Solomon, called Ecclesiastes, which at great length brings all earthly things into utter contempt. The book begins thus: "Vanity of the vain, saith the Preacher, vanity of the vain; all is vanity. What profit hath a man of all his labor which he taketh under the sun?" If all these words are considered, weighed, and thoroughly examined, many things are found of essential importance to those who seek to flee from the world and to take shelter in God; but this requires time and our discourse hastens on to other topics. But, after this beginning, he goes on to show in detail that the vain are

those who are deceived by things of this sort; and he calls this which deceives them vanity,—not that God did not create those things, but because men choose to subject themselves by their sins to those things, which the divine law has made subject to them in well-doing. For when you consider things beneath yourself to be admirable and desirable, what is this but to be cheated and misled by unreal goods? The man, then, who is temperate in such mortal and transient things has his rule of life confirmed by both Testaments, that he should love none of these things, nor think them desirable for their own sakes, but should use them as far as is required for the purposes and duties of life, with the moderation of an employer instead of the ardor of a lover. These remarks on temperance are few in proportion to the greatness of the theme, but perhaps too many in view of the task on hand.

Chapter 22.—Fortitude Comes from the Love of God.

40. On fortitude we must be brief. The love, then, of which we speak, which ought with all sanctity to burn in desire for God, is called temperance, in not seeking for earthly things, and fortitude in bearing the loss of them. But among all things which are possessed in this life, the body is, by God's most righteous laws, for the sin of old, man's heaviest bond, which is well known as a fact but most incomprehensible in its mystery. Lest this bond should be shaken and disturbed, the soul is shaken with the fear of toil and pain; lest it should be lost and destroyed, the soul is shaken with the fear of death. For the soul loves it from the force of habit, not knowing that by using it well and wisely its resurrection and

reformation will, by the divine help and decree, be without any trouble made subject to its authority. But when the soul turns to God wholly in this love, it knows these things, and so will not only disregard death, but will even desire it.

41. Then there is the great struggle with pain. But there is nothing, though of iron hardness, which the fire of love cannot subdue. And when the mind is carried up to God in this love, it will soar above all torture free and glorious, with wings beauteous and unhurt, on which chaste love rises to the embrace of God. Otherwise God must allow the lovers of gold, the lovers of praise, the lovers of women, to have more fortitude than the lovers of Himself, though love in those cases is rather to be called passion or lust. And yet even here we may see with what force the mind presses on with unflagging energy, despite all alarms, towards that it loves; and we learn that we should bear all things rather than forsake God, since those men bear so much in order to forsake Him.

Chapter 23.—Scripture Precepts and Examples of Fortitude.

42. Instead of quoting here authorities from the New Testament, where it is said, "Tribulation worketh patience; and patience, experience and experience, hope;" and where, in addition to these words, there is proof and confirmation of them from the example of those who spoke them; I will rather summon an example of patience from the Old Testament, against which the Manichæans make fierce assaults. Nor will I refer to the man who, amid great bodily suffering, and with a dreadful disease in his limbs, not only bore human evils, but discoursed of

things divine. Whoever gives considerate attention to the utterances of this man, will learn from every one of them what value is to be attached to those things which men try to keep in their power, and in so doing are themselves brought by passion into bondage, so that they become the slaves of mortal things, while seeking ignorantly to be their masters. This man, in the loss of all his wealth, and on being suddenly reduced to the greatest poverty, kept his mind so unshaken and fixed upon God, as to manifest that these things were not great in his view, but that he was great in relation to them, and God to him. If this mind were to be found in men in our day, we should not be so strongly cautioned in the New Testament against the possession of these things in order that we may be perfect; for to have these things without cleaving to them is much more admirable than not to have them at all.

43. But since we are speaking here of bearing pain and bodily sufferings, I pass from this man, great as he was, indomitable as he was: this is the case of a man. But these Scriptures present to me a woman of amazing fortitude, and I must at once go on to her case. This woman, along with seven children, allowed the tyrant and executioner to extract her vitals from her body rather than a profane word from her mouth, encouraging her sons by her exhortations, though she suffered in the tortures of their bodies, and was herself to undergo what she called on them to bear. What patience could be greater than this? And yet why should we be astonished that the love of God, implanted in her inmost heart, bore up against tyrant, and executioner, and pain, and sex, and natural affection? Had she not heard, "Precious in the sight of the Lord is the death of His saints?" Had she not heard, "A patient man is better than the mightiest?" Had she not

heard, "All that is appointed thee receive; and in pain bear it; and in abasement keep thy patience: for in fire are gold and silver tried?" Had she not heard, "The fire tries the vessels of the potter, and for just men is the trial of tribulation?" These she knew, and many other precepts of fortitude written in these books, which alone existed at that time, by the same divine Spirit who writes those in the New Testament.

Chapter 24.—Of Justice and Prudence.

44. What of justice that pertains to God? As the Lord says, "Ye cannot serve two masters," and the apostle denounces those who serve the creature rather than the Creator, was it not said before in the Old Testament, "Thou shalt worship the Lord thy God, and Him only shalt thou serve?" I need say no more on this, for these books are full of such passages. The lover, then, whom we are describing, will get from justice this rule of life, that he must with perfect readiness serve the God whom he loves, the highest good, the highest wisdom, the highest peace; and about all other things, must either rule them as subject to himself, or treat them with a view to their subjection. This rule of life, is, as we have shown, confirmed by the authority of both Testaments.

45. With equal brevity we must treat of prudence, to which it belongs to discern between what is to be desired and what to be shunned. Without this, nothing can be done of what we have already spoken of. It is the part of prudence to keep watch with most anxious vigilance, lest any evil influence should stealthily creep in upon us. Thus the Lord often exclaims, "Watch;" and He says, "Walk while ye have the light, lest darkness come

upon you." And then it is said, "Know ye not that a little leaven leavens the whole lump?" And no passage can be quoted from the Old Testament more expressly condemning this mental somnolence, which makes us insensible to destruction advancing on us step by step, than those words of the prophet, "He who despises small things shall fall by degrees." On this topic I might discourse at length did our haste allow of it. And did our present task demand it, we might perhaps prove the depth of these mysteries, by making a mock of which profane men in their perfect ignorance fall, not certainly by degrees, but with a headlong overthrow.

Chapter 25.—Four Moral Duties Regarding the Love of God, of Which Love the Reward is Eternal Life and the Knowledge of the Truth.

46. I need say no more about right conduct. For if God is man's chief good, which you cannot deny, it clearly follows, since to seek the chief good is to live well, that to live well is nothing else but to love God with all the heart, with all the soul, with all the mind; and, as arising from this, that this love must be preserved entire and incorrupt, which is the part of temperance; that it give way before no troubles, which is the part of fortitude; that it serve no other, which is the part of justice; that it be watchful in its inspection of things lest craft or fraud steal in, which is the part of prudence. This is the one perfection of man, by which alone he can succeed in attaining to the purity of truth. This both Testaments enjoin in concert; this is commended on both sides alike. Why do you continue to cast reproaches on Scriptures of which you are ignorant? Do you not see the folly of your

attack upon books which only those who do not understand them find fault with, and which only those who find fault fail in understanding? For neither can an enemy know them, nor can one who knows them be other than a friend to them.

47. Let us then, as many as have in view to reach eternal life, love God with all the heart, with all the soul, with all the mind. For eternal life contains the whole reward in the promise of which we rejoice; nor can the reward precede desert, nor be given to a man before he is worthy of it. What can be more unjust than this, and what is more just than God? We should not then demand the reward before we deserve to get it. Here, perhaps, it is not out of place to ask what is eternal life; or rather let us hear the Bestower of it: "This," He says, "is life eternal, that they should know Thee, the true God, and Jesus Christ whom Thou hast sent." So eternal life is the knowledge of the truth. See, then, how perverse and preposterous is the character of those who think that their teaching of the knowledge of God will make us perfect, when this is the reward of those already perfect! What else, then, have we to do but first to love with full affection Him whom we desire to know? Hence arises that principle on which we have all along insisted, that there is nothing more wholesome in the Catholic Church than using authority before argument.

Chapter 26.—Love of Ourselves and of Our Neighbor.

48. To proceed to what remains. It may be thought that there is nothing here about man himself, the lover. But to think this, shows a want of clear perception. For it is impossible for one who loves God not to love himself. For he alone has a proper love for himself who aims diligently at the attainment of the chief and true good; and if this is nothing else but God, as has been shown, what is to prevent one who loves God from loving himself? And then, among men should there be no bond of mutual love? Yea, verily; so that we can think of no surer step towards the love of God than the love of man to man.

49. Let the Lord then supply us with the other precept in answer to the question about the precepts of life; for He was not satisfied with one as knowing that God is one thing and man another, and that the difference is nothing less than that between the Creator and the thing created in the likeness of its Creator. He says then that the second precept is, "Thou shalt love thy neighbor as thyself." Now you love yourself suitably when you love God better than yourself. What, then, you aim at in yourself you must aim at in your neighbor, namely, that he may love God with a perfect affection. For you do not love him as yourself, unless you try to draw him to that good which you are yourself pursuing. For this is the one good which has room for all to pursue it along with thee. From this precept proceed the duties of human society, in which it is hard to keep from error. But the first thing to aim at is, that we should be benevolent, that is, that we cherish no malice and no evil design against another. For

man is the nearest neighbor of man.

50. Hear also what Paul says: "The love of our neighbor," he says, "worketh no ill." The testimonies here made use of are very short, but, if I mistake not, they are to the point, and sufficient for the purpose. And everyone knows how many and how weighty are the words to be found everywhere in these books on the love of our neighbor. But as a man may sin against another in two ways, either by injuring him or by not helping him when it is in his power, and as it is for these things which no loving man would do that men are called wicked, all that is required is, I think, proved by these words, "The love of our neighbor worketh no ill." And if we cannot attain to good unless we first desist from working evil, our love of our neighbor is a sort of cradle of our love to God, so that, as it is said, "the love of our neighbor worketh no ill," we may rise from this to these other words, "We know that all things issue in good to them that love God."

51. But there is a sense in which these either rise together to fullness and perfection, or, while the love of God is first in beginning, the love of our neighbor is first in coming to perfection. For perhaps divine love takes hold on us more rapidly at the outset, but we reach perfection more easily in lower things. However that may be, the main point is this, that no one should think that while he despises his neighbor he will come to happiness and to the God whom he loves. And would that it were as easy to seek the good of our neighbor, or to avoid hurting him, as it is for one well trained and kind-hearted to love his neighbor! These things require more than mere good-will, and can be done only by a high degree of thoughtfulness and prudence, which belongs only to those to whom it is given by God, the source of all good. On

this topic—which is one, I think, of great difficulty—I will try to say a few words such as my plan admits of, resting all my hope in Him whose gifts these are.

Chapter 27.—On Doing Good to the Body of Our Neighbor.

52. Man, then, as viewed by his fellow-man, is a rational soul with a mortal and earthly body in its service. Therefore he who loves his neighbor does good partly to the man's body, and partly to his soul. What benefits the body is called medicine; what benefits the soul, discipline. Medicine here includes everything that either preserves or restores bodily health. It includes, therefore, not only what belongs to the art of medical men, properly so called, but also food and drink, clothing and shelter, and every means of covering and protection to guard our bodies against injuries and mishaps from without as well as from within. For hunger and thirst, and cold and heat, and all violence from without, produce loss of that health which is the point to be considered.

53. Hence those who seasonably and wisely supply all the things required for warding off these evils and distresses are called compassionate, although they may have been so wise that no painful feeling disturbed their mind in the exercise of compassion. No doubt the word compassionate implies suffering in the heart of the man who feels for the sorrow of another. And it is equally true that a wise man ought to be free from all painful emotion when he assists the needy, when he gives food to the hungry and water to the thirsty, when he clothes the naked, when he takes the stranger into his house, when he sets free the oppressed, when, lastly, he

extends his charity to the dead in giving them burial. Still the epithet compassionate is a proper one, although he acts with tranquility of mind, not from the stimulus of painful feeling, but from motives of benevolence. There is no harm in the word compassionate when there is no passion in the case.

54. Fools, again, who avoid the exercise of compassion as a vice, because they are not sufficiently moved by a sense of duty without feeling also distressful emotion, are frozen into hard insensibility, which is very different from the calm of a rational serenity. God, on the other hand, is properly called compassionate; and the sense in which He is so will be understood by those whom piety and diligence have made fit to understand. There is a danger lest, in using the words of the learned, we harden the souls of the unlearned by leading them away from compassion instead of softening them with the desire of a charitable disposition. As compassion, then, requires us to ward off these distresses from others, so harmlessness forbids the infliction of them.

Chapter 28.—On Doing Good to the Soul of Our Neighbor. Two Parts of Discipline, Restraint and Instruction. Through Good Conduct We Arrive at the Knowledge of the Truth.

55. About discipline, by which the health of the mind is restored, without which bodily health avails nothing for security against misery, the subject is one of great difficulty. And as in the body we said it is one thing to cure diseases and wounds, which few can do properly, and another thing to meet the cravings of hunger and thirst, and to give assistance in all the other ways in which

any man may at any time help another; so in the mind there are some things in which the high and rare offices of the teacher are not much called for,—as, for instance, in advice and exhortation to give to the needy the things already mentioned as required for the body. To give such advice is to aid the mind by discipline, as giving the things themselves is aiding the body by our resources. But there are other cases where diseases of the mind, many and various in kind, are healed in a way strange and indescribable. Unless His medicine were sent from heaven to men, so heedlessly do they go on in sin, there would be no hope of salvation; and, indeed, even bodily health, if you go to the root of the matter, can have come to men from none but God, who gives to all things their being and their well-being.

56. This discipline, then, which is the medicine of the mind, as far as we can gather from the sacred Scriptures, includes two things, restraint and instruction. Restraint implies fear, and instruction love, in the person benefited by the discipline; for in the giver of the benefit there is the love without the fear. In both of these God Himself, by whose goodness and mercy it is that we are anything, has given us in the two Testaments a rule of discipline. For though both are found in both Testaments, still fear is prominent in the Old, and love in the New; which the apostle calls bondage in the one, and liberty in the other. Of the marvelous order and divine harmony of these Testaments it would take long to speak, and many pious and learned men have discoursed on it. The theme demands many books to set it forth and explain it as far as is possible for man. He, then, who loves his neighbor endeavors all he can to procure his safety in body and in soul, making the health of the mind the standard in his

treatment of the body. And as regards the mind, his endeavors are in this order, that he should first fear and then love God. This is true excellence of conduct, and thus the knowledge of the truth is acquired which we are ever in the pursuit of.

57. The Manichæans agree with me as regards the duty of loving God and our neighbor, but they deny that this is taught in the Old Testament. How greatly they err in this is, I think, clearly shown by the passages quoted above on both these duties. But, in a single word, and one which only stark madness can oppose, do they not see the unreasonableness of denying that these very two precepts which they commend are quoted by the Lord in the Gospel from the Old Testament, "Thou shalt love the Lord thy God with all thy heart, and with all thy soul, and with all thy mind;" and the other, "Thou shalt love thy neighbor as thyself?" Or if they dare not deny this, from the light of truth being too strong for them, let them deny that these precepts are salutary; let them deny, if they can, that they teach the best morality; let them assert that it is not a duty to love God, or to love our neighbor; that all things do not issue in good to them that love God; that it is not true that the love of our neighbor worketh no ill (a two-fold regulation of human life which is most salutary and excellent). By such assertions they cut themselves off not only from Christians, but from mankind. But if they dare not speak thus, but must confess the divinity of the precepts, why do they not desist from assailing and maligning with horrible profanity the books from which they are quoted?

58. Will they say, as they often do, that although we find these precepts in the books, it does not follow that all is good that is found there? How to meet and refute

this quibble I do not well see. Shall I discuss the words of the Old Testament one by one, to prove to stubborn and ignorant men their perfect agreement with the New Testament? But when will this be done? When shall I have time, or they patience? What, then, is to be done? Shall I desert the cause, and leave them to escape detection in an opinion which, though false and impious, is hard to disprove? I will not. God will Himself be at hand to aid me; nor will He suffer me in those straits to remain helpless or forsaken.

Chapter 29.—Of the Authority of the Scriptures.

59. Attend, then, ye Manichæans, if perchance there are some of you of whom your superstition has hold so as to allow you yet to escape. Attend, I say, without obstinacy, without the desire to oppose, otherwise your decision will be fatal to yourselves. No one can doubt, and you are not so lost to the truth as not to understand that if it is good, as all allow, to love God and our neighbor, whatever hangs on these two precepts cannot rightly be pronounced bad. What it is that hangs on them it would be absurd to think of learning from me. Hear Christ Himself; hear Christ, I say; hear the Wisdom of God: "On these two commandments," He says, "hang all the law and the prophets."

60. What can the most shameless obstinacy say to this? That these are not Christ's words? But they are written in the Gospel as His words. That the writing is false? Is not this most profane blasphemy? Is it not most presumptuous to speak thus? Is it not most foolhardy? Is it not most criminal? The worshippers of idols, who hate even the name of Christ, never dared to speak thus against

these Scriptures. For the utter overthrow of all literature will follow, and there will be an end to all books handed down from the past, if what is supported by such a strong popular belief and established by the uniform testimony of so many men and so many times, is brought into such suspicion, that it is not allowed to have the credit and the authority of common history. In fine, what can you quote from any writings of which I may not speak in this way if it is quoted against my opinion and my purpose?

61. And is it not intolerable that they forbid us to believe a book widely known and placed now in the hands of all, while they insist on our believing the book which they quote? If any writing is to be suspected, what should be more so than one which has not merited notoriety, or which may be throughout a forgery, bearing a false name? If you force such a writing on me against my will, and make a display of authority to drive me into belief, shall I, when I have a writing which I see spread far and wide for a length of time, and sanctioned by the concordant testimony of churches scattered over all the world, degrade myself by doubting, and, worse degradation, by doubting at your suggestion? Even if you brought forward other readings, I should not receive them unless supported by general agreement; and this being the case, do you think that now, when you bring forward nothing to compare with the text except your own silly and inconsiderate statement, mankind are so unreasonable and so forsaken by divine Providence as to prefer to those Scriptures not others quoted by you in refutation, but merely your own words? You ought to bring forward another manuscript with the same contents, but incorrupt and more correct, with only the passage wanting which you charge with being spurious. For example, if you hold

that the Epistle of Paul to the Romans is spurious, you must bring forward another incorrupt, or rather another manuscript with the same epistle of the same apostle, free from error and corruption. You say you will not, lest you be suspected of corrupting it. This is your usual reply, and a true one. Were you to do this, we should assuredly have this very suspicion; and all men of any sense would have it too. See then what you are to think of your own authority; and consider whether it is right to believe your words against these Scriptures, when the simple fact that a manuscript is brought forward by you makes it dangerous to put faith in it.

Chapter 30.—The Church Apostrophized as Teacher of All Wisdom. Doctrine of the Catholic Church.

62. But why say more on this? For who but sees that men who dare to speak thus against the Christian Scriptures, though they may not be what they are suspected of being, are at least no Christians? For to Christians this rule of life is given, that we should love the Lord Our God with all the heart, with all the soul, and with all the mind, and our neighbor as ourselves; for on these two commandments hang all the law and the prophets. Rightly, then, Catholic Church, most true mother of Christians, dost thou not only teach that God alone, to find whom is the happiest life, must be worshipped in perfect purity and chastity, bringing in no creature as an object of adoration whom we should be required to serve; and from that incorrupt and inviolable eternity to which alone man should be made subject, in cleaving to which alone the rational soul escapes misery, excluding everything made, everything liable to change,

everything under the power of time; without confounding what eternity, and truth, and peace itself keeps separate, or separating what a common majesty unites: but thou dost also contain love and charity to our neighbor in such a way, that for all kinds of diseases with which souls are for their sins afflicted, there is found with thee a medicine of prevailing efficacy.

    63. Thy training and teaching are childlike for children, forcible for youths, peaceful for the aged, considering the age of the mind as well as of the body. Thou subjects women to their husbands in chaste and faithful obedience, not to gratify passion, but for the propagation of offspring, and for domestic society. Thou gives to men authority over their wives, not to mock the weaker sex, but in the laws of unfeigned love. Thou dost subordinate children to their parents in a kind of free bondage, and dost set parents over their children in a godly rule. Thou binds brothers to brothers in a religious tie stronger and closer than that of blood. Without violation of the connections of nature and of choice, thou brings within the bond of mutual love every relationship of kindred, and every alliance of affinity. Thou teaches servants to cleave to their masters from delight in their task rather than from the necessity of their position. Thou renders masters forbearing to their servants, from a regard to God their common Master, and more disposed to advise than to compel. Thou unite citizen to citizen, nation to nation, yea, man to man, from the recollection of their first parents, not only in society but in fraternity. Thou teaches kings to seek the good of their peoples; thou counsels peoples to be subject to their kings. Thou teaches carefully to whom honor is due, to whom regard, to whom reverence, to whom fear, to whom con solation,

to whom admonition, to whom encouragement, to whom discipline, to whom rebuke, to whom punishment; showing both how all are not due to all, and how to all love is due, and how injury is due to none.

64. Then, after this human love has nourished and invigorated the mind cleaving to thy breast, and fitted it for following God, when the divine majesty has begun to disclose itself as far as suffices for man while a dweller on the earth, such fervent charity is produced, and such a flame of divine love is kindled, that by the burning out of all vices, and by the purification and sanctification of the man, it becomes plain how divine are these words, "I am a consuming fire," and, "I have come to send fire on the earth." These two utterances of one God stamped on both Testaments, exhibit with harmonious testimony, the sanctification of the soul, pointing forward to the accomplishment of that which is also quoted in the New Testament from the Old: "Death is swallowed up in victory. O death, where is thy sting? Where, O death, is thy contest?" Could these heretics understand this one saying, no longer proud but quite reconciled, they would worship God nowhere but with thee and in thy bosom. In thee, as is fit, divine precepts are kept by widely-scattered multitudes. In thee, as is fit, it is well understood how much more heinous sin is when the law is known than when it is unknown. For "the sting of death is sin, and the strength of sin is the law," which adds to the force with which the consciousness of disregard of the precept strikes and slays. In thee it is seen, as is fit, how vain is effort under the law, when lust lays waste the mind, and is held in check by fear of punishment, instead of being overborne by the love of virtue. Thine, as is fit, are the many hospitable, the many friendly, the many

compassionate, the many learned, the many chaste, the many saints, the many so ardent in their love to God, that in perfect continence and amazing indifference to this world they find happiness even in solitude.

Chapter 31.—The Life of the Anachoretes and Cœnobites Set Against the Continence of the Manichæans.

65. What must we think is seen by those who can live without seeing their fellow creatures, though not without loving them? It must be something transcending human things in contemplating which man can live without seeing his fellow-man. Hear now, ye Manichæans, the customs and notable continence of perfect Christians, who have thought it right not only to praise but also to practice the height of chastity, that you may be restrained, if there is any shame in you, from vaunting your abstinence before uninstructed minds as if it were the hardest of all things. I will speak of things of which you are not ignorant, though you hide them from us. For who does not know that there is a daily increasing multitude of Christian men of absolute continence spread all over the world, especially in the East and in Egypt, as you cannot help knowing?

66. I will say nothing of those to whom I just now alluded, who, in complete seclusion from the view of men, inhabit regions utterly barren, content with simple bread, which is brought to them periodically, and with water, enjoying communion with God, to whom in purity of mind they cleave, and most blessed in contemplating His beauty, which can be seen only by the understanding of saints. I will say nothing of them, because some

people think them to have abandoned human things more than they ought, not considering how much those may benefit us in their minds by prayer, and in their lives by example, whose bodies we are not permitted to see. But to discuss this point would take long, and would be fruitless; for if a man does not of his own accord regard this high pitch of sanctity as admirable and honorable, how can our speaking lead him to do so? Only the Manichæans, who make a boast of nothing, should be reminded that the abstinence and continence of the great saints of the Catholic Church has gone so far, that some think it should be checked and recalled within the limits of humanity,—so far above men, even in the judgment of those who disapprove, have their minds soared.

67. But if this is beyond our tolerance, who can but admire and commend those who, slighting and discarding the pleasures of this world, living together in a most chaste and holy society, unite in passing their time in prayers, in readings, in discussions, without any swelling of pride, or noise of contention, or sullenness of envy; but quiet, modest, peaceful, their life is one of perfect harmony and devotion to God, an offering most acceptable to Him from whom the power to do those things is obtained? No one possesses anything of his own; no one is a burden to another. They work with their hands in such occupations as may feed their bodies without distracting their minds from God. The product of their toil they give to the decans or tithesmen,—so called from being set over the tithes,—so that no one is occupied with the care of his body, either in food or clothes, or in anything else required for daily use or for the common ailments. These decans, again, arranging everything with great care, and meeting promptly the demands made by

that life because bodily infirmities, have one called "father," to whom they give in their accounts. These fathers are not only saintlier in their conduct, but also distinguished for divine learning, and of high character in every way; and without pride they superintend those whom they call their children, having themselves great authority in giving orders, and meeting with willing obedience from those under their charge. At the close of the day they assemble from their separate dwellings before their meal to hear their father, assembling to the number of three thousand at least for one father; for one may have even a much larger number than this. They listen with astonishing eagerness in perfect silence, and give expression to the feelings of their minds as moved by the words of the preacher, in groans, or tears, or signs of joy without noise or shouting. Then there is refreshment for the body, as much as health and a sound condition of the body requires, everyone checking unlawful appetite, so as not to go to excess even in the poor, inexpensive fare provided. So they not only abstain from flesh and wine, in order to gain the mastery over their passions, but also from those things which are only the more likely to whet the appetite of the palate and of the stomach, from what some call their greater cleanness, which often serves as a ridiculous and disgraceful excuse for an unseemly taste for exquisite viands, as distant from animal food. Whatever they possess in addition to what is required for their support (and much is obtained, owing to their industry and frugality), they distribute to the needy with greater care than they took in procuring it for themselves. For while they make no effort to obtain abundance, they make every effort to prevent their abundance remaining with them,—so much so, that they send shiploads to places inhabited by poor people. I need say no more on a matter known to all.

68. Such, too, is the life of the women, who serve God assiduously and chastely, living apart and removed as far as propriety demands from the men, to whom they are united only in pious affection and in imitation of virtue. No young men are allowed access to them, nor even old men, however respectable and approved, except to the porch, in order to furnish necessary supplies. For the women occupy and maintain themselves by working in wool, and hand over the cloth to the brethren, from whom, in return, they get what they need for food. Such customs, such a life, such arrangements, such a system, I could not commend as it deserves, if I wished to commend it; besides, I am afraid that it would seem as if I thought it unlikely to gain acceptance from the mere description of it, if I considered myself obliged to add an ornamental eulogium to the simple narrative. Ye Manichæans, find fault here if you can. Do not bring into prominence our tares before men too blind to discriminate.

Chapter 32.—Praise of the Clergy.

69. There is not, however, such narrowness in the moral excellence of the Catholic Church as that I should limit my praise of it to the life of those here mentioned. For how many bishops have I known most excellent and holy men, how many presbyters, how many deacons, and ministers of all kinds of the divine sacraments, whose virtue seems to me more admirable and worthier of commendation because the greater difficulty of preserving it amidst the manifold varieties of men, and in this life of

turmoil! For they preside over men needing cure as much as over those already cured. The vices of the crowd must be borne with in order that they may be cured, and the plague must be endured before it is subdued. To keep here the best way of life and a mind calm and peaceful is very hard. Here, in a word, we are among people who are learning to live. There they live.

Chapter 33.—Another Kind of Men Living Together in Cities. Fasts of Three Days.

70. Still I would not on this account cast a slight upon a praiseworthy class of Christians,—those, namely, who live together in cities, quite apart from common life. I saw at Milan a lodging-house of saints, in number not a few, presided over by one presbyter, a man of great excellence and learning. At Rome I knew several places where there was in each one eminent for weight of character, and prudence, and divine knowledge, presiding over all the rest who lived with him, in Christian charity, and sanctity, and liberty. These, too, are not burdensome to anyone; but, in the Eastern fashion, and on the authority of the Apostle Paul, they maintain themselves with their own hands. I was told that many practiced fasts of quite amazing severity, not merely taking only one meal daily towards night, which is everywhere quite common, but very often continuing for three days or more in succession without food or drink. And this among not men only, but women, who also live together in great numbers as widows or virgins, gaining a livelihood by spinning and weaving, and presided over in each case by a woman of the greatest judgment and experience, skilled and accomplished not only in directing and forming moral

conduct, but also in instructing the understanding.

71. With all this, no one is pressed to endure hardships for which he is unfit; nothing is imposed on any one against his will; nor is he condemned by the rest because he confesses himself too feeble to imitate them: for they bear in mind how strongly Scripture enjoins charity on all: they bear in mind "To the pure all things are pure," and "Not that which entered into your mouth defiled you, but that which cometh out of it." Accordingly, all their endeavors are concerned not about the rejection of kinds of food as polluted, but about the subjugation of inordinate desire and the maintenance of brotherly love. They remember, "Meats for the belly, and the belly for meats; but God shall destroy both it and them;" and again, "Neither if we eat shall we abound, nor if we refrain from eating shall we be in want;" and, above all, this: "It is good, my brethren, not to eat flesh, nor drink wine, nor anything whereby thy brother is offended;" for this passage shows that love is the end to be aimed at in all these things. "For one man," he says, "believes that he can eat all things: another, who is weak, eats herbs. He that eats, let him not despise him that eats not; and let not him that eats not judge him that eats: for God hath approved him. Who art thou that thou shouldest judge another man's servant? To his own master he stands or fails; but he shall stand: for God is able to make him to stand." And a little after: "He that eats, to the Lord he eats, and giveth God thanks; and he that eats not, to the Lord he eats not, and giveth God thanks." And also in what follows: "So every one of us shall give account of himself to God. Let us not, then, any more judge one another: but judge this rather, that ye place no stumbling-block, or cause of offence, in the way of a brother. I

know, and am confident in the Lord Jesus, that there is nothing common in itself: but to him that thinketh anything to be common, to him it is common." Could he have shown better that it is not in the things we eat, but in the mind, that there is a power able to pollute it, and therefore that even those who are fit to think lightly of these things, and know perfectly that they are not polluted if they take any food in mental superiority, without being gluttons, should still have regard to charity? See what he adds: "For if thy brother be grieved with thy meat, now walks thou not charitably."

72. Read the rest: it is too long to quote all. You will find that those able to think lightly of such things,— that is, those of greater strength and stability,—are told that they must nevertheless abstain, lest those should be offended who from their weakness are still in need of such abstinence. The people I was describing know and observe these things; for they are Christians, not heretics. They understand Scripture according to the apostolic teaching, not according to the presumptuous and fictitious name of apostle. Him that eats not no one despises; him that eats no one judges; he who is weak eats herbs. Many who are strong, however, do this for the sake of the weak; with many the reason for so doing is not this, but that they may have a cheaper diet, and may lead a life of the greatest tranquility, with the least expensive provision for the support of the body. "For all things are lawful for me," he says; "but I will not be brought under the power of any." Thus many do not eat flesh, and yet do not superstitiously regard it as unclean. And so the same people who abstain when in health take it when unwell without any fear, if it is required as a cure. Many drink no wine; but they do not think that wine defiles them; for

they cause it to be given with the greatest propriety and moderation to people of languid temperament, and, in short, to all who cannot have bodily health without it. When some foolishly refuse it, they counsel them as brothers not to let a silly superstition make them weaker instead of making them holier. They read to them the apostle's precept to his disciple to "take a little wine for his many infirmities." Then they diligently exercise piety; bodily exercise, they know, profited for a short time, as the same apostle says.

73. Those, then who are able, and they are without number, abstain both from flesh and from wine for two reasons: either for the weakness of their brethren, or for their own liberty. Charity is principally attended to. There is charity in their choice of diet, charity in their speech, charity in their dress, charity in their looks. Charity is the point where they meet, and the plan by which they act. To transgress against charity is thought criminal, like transgressing against God. Whatever opposes this is attacked and expelled; whatever injures it is not allowed to continue for a single day. They know that it has been so enjoined by Christ and the apostles; that without it all things are empty, with it all are fulfilled.

Chapter 34.—The Church is Not to Be Blamed for the Conduct of Bad Christians, Worshippers of Tombs and Pictures.

74. Make objections against these, ye Manichæans, if you can. Look at these people, and speak of them reproachfully, if you dare, without falsehood. Compare their fasts with your fasts, their chastity with yours; compare them to yourselves in dress, food, self-

restraint, and, lastly, in charity. Compare, which is most to the point, their precepts with yours. Then you will see the difference between show and sincerity, between the right way and the wrong, between faith and imposture, between strength and inflatedness, between happiness and wretchedness, between unity and disunion; in short, between the sirens of superstition and the harbor of religion.

75. Do not summon against me professors of the Christian name, who neither know nor give evidence of the power of their profession. Do not hunt up the numbers of ignorant people, who even in the true religion are superstitious, or are so given up to evil passions as to forget what they have promised to God. I know that there are many worshippers of tombs and pictures. I know that there are many who drink to great excess over the dead, and who, in the feasts which they make for corpses, bury themselves over the buried, and give to their gluttony and drunkenness the name of religion. I know that there are many who in words have renounced this world, and yet desire to be burdened with all the weight of worldly things, and rejoice in such burdens. Nor is it surprising that among so many multitudes you should find some by condemning whose life you may deceive the unwary and seduce them from Catholic safety; for in your small numbers you are at a loss when called on to show even one out of those whom you call the elect who keeps the precepts, which in your indefensible superstition you profess. How silly those are, how impious, how mischievous, and to what extent they are neglected by most, nearly all of you, I have shown in another volume.

76. My advice to you now is this: that you should at least desist from slandering the Catholic Church, by

declaiming against the conduct of men whom the Church herself condemns, seeking daily to correct them as wicked children. Then, if any of them by good will and by the help of God are corrected, they regain by repentance what they had lost by sin. Those, again, who with wicked will persist in their old vices, or even add to them others still worse, are indeed allowed to remain in the field of the Lord, and to grow along with the good seed; but the time for separating the tares will come. Or if, from their having at least the Christian name, they are to be placed among the chaff rather than among thistles, there will also come One to purge the floor and to separate the chaff from the wheat, and to assign to each part (according to its desert) the due reward.

Chapter 35.—Marriage and Property Allowed to the Baptized by the Apostles.

77. Meanwhile, why do you rage? why does party spirit blind your eyes? Why do you entangle yourselves in a long defense of such great error? Seek for fruit in the field, seek for wheat in the floor: they will be found easily, and will present themselves to the inquirer. Why do you look so exclusively at the dross? Why do you use the roughness of the hedge to scare away the inexperienced from the fatness of the garden? There is a proper entrance, though known to but a few; and by it men come in, though you disbelieve it, or do not wish to find it. In the Catholic Church there are believers without number who do not use the world, and there are those who "use it," in the words of the apostle, "as not using it," as was proved in those times when Christians were forced to worship idols. For then, how many wealthy men, how

many peasant householders, how many merchants, how many military men, how many leading men in their own cities, and how many senators, people of both sexes, giving up all these empty and transitory things, though while they used them they were not bound down by them, endured death for the salutary faith and religion, and proved to unbelievers that instead of being possessed by all these things they really possessed them?

78. Why do you reproach us by saying that men renewed in baptism ought no longer to beget children, or to possess fields, and houses, and money? Paul allows it. For, as cannot be denied, he wrote to believers, after recounting many kinds of evil-doers who shall not possess the kingdom of God: "And such were you," he says: "but ye are washed, but ye are sanctified, but ye are justified in the name of the Lord Jesus Christ and by the Spirit of our God." By the washed and sanctified, no one, assuredly, will venture to think any are meant but believers, and those who have renounced this world. But, after showing to whom he writes, let us see whether he allows these things to them. He goes on: "All things are lawful for me, but all things are not expedient: all things are lawful for me, but I will not be brought under the power of any. Meat for the belly, and the belly for meats: but God will destroy both it and them. Now the body is not for fornication, but for the Lord, and the Lord for the body. But God raised up the Lord, and will raise us up also by His own power. Know ye not that your bodies are the members of Christ? shall I then take the members of Christ, and make them the members of a harlot? God forbid. Know ye not that he which is joined to a harlot is made one body? for the twain, saith He, shall be one flesh. But he that is joined to the Lord is one spirit. Flee

fornication. Whatever sin a man doeth is without the body: but he that committed fornication sinned against his own body. Know ye not that your members are the temple of the Holy Spirit which is in you, which ye have of God, and ye are not your own? For ye are bought with a great price: glorify God, and carry Him in your body."
"But of the things concerning which ye wrote to me: it is good for a man not to touch a woman. Nevertheless, to avoid fornication, let every man have his own wife, and let every woman have her own husband. Let the husband render unto the wife due benevolence: and likewise also the wife unto the husband. The wife hath not power of her own body, but the husband: and likewise also the husband hath not power of his own body, but the wife. Defraud ye not one the other, except it be with consent for a time, that ye may have leisure for prayer; and come together again, that Satan tempt you not for your incontinency. But I speak this by permission, and not of commandment. For I would that all men were even as I myself: but every man hath his proper gift of God, one after this manner, and another after that."

79. Has the apostle, think you, both shown sufficiently to the strong what is highest, and permitted to the weaker what is next best? Not to touch a woman he shows is highest when he says, "I would that all men were even as I myself." But next to this highest is conjugal chastity, that man may not be the prey of fornication. Did he say that these people were not yet believers because they were married? Indeed, by this conjugal chastity he says that those who are united are sanctified by one another, if one of them is an unbeliever, and that their children also are sanctified. "The unbelieving husband," he says, "is sanctified by the believing wife, and the

unbelieving woman by the believing husband: otherwise your children would be unclean; but now are they holy." Why do you persist in opposition to such plain truth? Why do you try to darken the light of Scripture by vain shadows?

80. Do not say that catechumens can have wives, but not believers; that catechumens may have money, but not believers. For there are many who use as not using. And in that sacred washing the renewal of the new man is begun so as gradually to reach perfection, in some more quickly, in others more slowly. The progress, however, to a new life is made in the case of many, if we view the matter without hostility, but attentively. As the apostle says of himself, "Though the outward man perish, the inward man is renewed day by day." The apostle says that the inward man is renewed day by day that it may reach perfection; and you wish it to begin with perfection! And it were well if you did wish it. In reality, you aim not at raising the weak, but at misleading the unwary. You ought not to have spoken so arrogantly, even if it were known that you are perfect in your childish precepts. But when your conscience knows that those whom you bring into your sect, when they come to a more intimate acquaintance with you, will find many things in you which nobody hearing you accuse others would suspect, is it not great impertinence to demand perfection in the weaker Catholics, to turn away the inexperienced from the Catholic Church, while you show nothing of the kind in yourself to those thus turned away? But not to seem to inveigh against you without reason, I will now close this volume, and will proceed at last to set forth the precepts of your life and your notable customs.

www.ingramcontent.com/pod-product-compliance
Lightning Source LLC
Chambersburg PA
CBHW052116070526
44584CB00017B/2511